White Silk Ribbons

Elin Pearce

BookLeaf Publishing

India | USA | UK

Presentation by *BookLeaf Publishing*

Web: www.bookleafpub.com

E-mail: info@bookleafpub.com

ISBN: 9789358737387

First edition 2023

To Agnetha Fältskog, Frida Lyngstad, Aileen Mclaughlin and TJ Davis, the childhood heroes in this book.

The Far End Of The Sky

In the absence of fairy tales, I can no longer
pretend,
I know we need to go to the universe' end.
To find a place that is exclusively ours,
I'll board Voyager 1 and travel to Mars.
My first stop is Mars' satellite,
on Phobos I imagine us lying in the melodious
moonlight,
but on the horizon, I can see Earth and all of my
fears.
Deimos reminds me of the demons behind all of
our tears.
I continue to fly through the asteroid belt,
their impact is reminiscent of the hurdles I've
felt.
So, I let Jupiter's gravity reign me in,
questioning whether this is somewhere we can
live without sin?
But I disregard the gas giant that glows in red,
its crushing presence fills me with dread.
I bypass Saturn's rings in favour of titan,
with the hope that this is a place that will
enlighten,
but it seems far too similar to our earth,

and neither Uranus or Titania can show your
worth.
Instead of Neptune, I detour through cinnamon
gold sequinned skies,
their colours remind me of your exquisite eyes.
As I continue to fly, I reach the Kuiper belt,
a place where it's only your heart I can melt.
Finally, I concede I am far enough away,
I can finally breathe, so here I will stay.
I'll let you choose between Haumea, Eris and
Pluto,
because I know out here that our love will grow.
We don't need to be illuminated by rays of
sunlight,
because deep in our hearts, we know, we are
right.

Diamond In The Sky

I am eternally indebted to the one who,
unknowingly, brought me back to a wonderful
life.
Last year, I lived in solitude,
drowning in spiralling thoughts.
When my head slipped under the water I'd drift
away.
In the absence of oxygen, I'd make my own,
wandering endlessly with her in forests
of emerald green.
We'd lay together in misty meadows,
staring at the scarlet skies.
We'd whisper under the faint twinkle of the stars
and she'd serenade me with harmonious
melodies
and I'd bask in her iridescent aura.
Her flawless velvety voice
served simultaneously as a barrier to the thorns
and an antidote to the pain.
She was there, grasping my hand
as I incubated in my chrysalis.
Now I'm out, without a doubt,
she sowed the seeds for my eclosion.
She transcribed my unspoken feelings
relentlessly,

patiently and tenderly until every road, every
avenue and every street
lead back to you.
She wrote your name in a thousand different
ways
and finally, she inscribed it on my heart.
For everything I'll be forever grateful
and her presence will always linger.
One day I'll thank her for taking me back to the
start.
My diamond in the sky.

The Poet

The writer in my heart spends her days
deliberating the ways,
she can tell you that she is
so in love with you.

I'll admit, she is quite dramatic.
Articulating love through intricate
alliterations and rhythmic rhymes.
Yet, if you can overlook the ostentatious frills
you'll see 'never leave me'.

She colours the world with words.
Amethyst skies and azure seas
born out of sunlight refraction,
but, if you can resist the distraction
you'll see 'you colour my world'.

She employs similes and metaphors,
the core of which convey
that love conquers all.
Behind the intricate veil
you'll see 'I need you by my side'.

I hope there will never be a reason to stop
spilling this ink.

Never grounds to stop weaving these words.
My heart is within the pages of your soul.
In reality, I am just writing and rewriting
you are 'the centre of my world;'.

Love Will Be The Death Of Me

I love, love.
I also hate, love.
Let's get this straight,
Cupid is not stupid.
He is a predator.
Savage.
Rapacious with a tenacious grip on his prey.
His prey being the innocent, the naive.
He starts by weaving the narrative of true love
and just when you being to trust,
That's when he begins to deceive.
Prancing around with his arrow,
turning it to nothing more than lust.
His perfect prey being those that dream
of twin flames twirling across poetic spheres.
Those desperate, for the formula of love.
Me.
I am a fool with these fictitious ideals.
The blood is slowly seeping out through
the wound in my heart.
Love will be the death of me.

Childhood Heroes

When I was a girl, I had career aspirations
and dreams of tropical vacations.
I had high expectations.
Now, a woman,
my heart is broken in places that can't be seen.
Merely a shell containing a clamour of
fragmented pieces.
My treasured memories have become eerie
echoes.
The girls at the centre of my memories have
become my heroes.
In their hands they hold shards of broken
promises and
splinters of my troubled dreams.
Their voices are nostalgic buttercups,
flowering amongst the thorns in my side.
When I am reminded that I am trapped,
an ocean on either side,
a smile from them is a slither of hope, to help
me cope.
A crescent moon, waxing into a previously
empty midnight sky.
I pray that I won't forever be reliant on these
illusions,
(no doubt some see them as delusions)
as sutures for my heart.

Sielvartas

Sielvartas, a Lithuanian word meaning,
tumbling of the soul.
The hole left by seemingly endless grief.
I believe a more appropriate word is crater, or
hollow.
The ease of life left with you and, some days,
I just want to follow.
I want to hear your voice once more.
Everyone tells me that it will take time,
but right now, it feels so raw.
Today, I phoned your landline.
I don't know what I expected of course,
it was no longer connected.
I feel so alone without you at the end of the
phone.
I just can't seem to accept
that you're no longer part of this world.
It's hard to put into words
but sometimes I feel like I can't breathe.
Once more I want to hear you say,
Nighty nighty naughty night.
The thing that scares me most,
is you've brought into sight,
the fact that life is too short.
It's not enough to exist,

I need to start taking risks.
It seems an impossible task without you by my
side
but, in the midnight sky,
I hope your star is glowing with pride.
I will love you forever.

Heaven is just a step away

I desired a blonde girl,
she was the sepia of falsified fantasy.
The productivity of puzzlement between love
and lust.
I trust the universe waved her my way
as a suggestion to ask myself questions.
As time passed her absence hurt.
So, instead I flirted with a glossy brunette.
Still, she was the sepia of falsified fantasy.
I genuinely believed she was,
the other half of my sanity.
I imagined that she was the girl in which I could
confide,
(I naively convinced myself that with some sexy
lingerie,
she could be swayed to my side).
Now, my heart is beating in the paint of honeyed
lies.
I now know that both my blonde and brunette
were lust disguised in a cloak of love.
I am choking on the realisation
that my flirtation no longer craves a girl in sepia.

White Silk Ribbons

I find myself lost in my childhood playground.
Drowned in feelings I can't comprehend,
my thoughts are spinning around,
I feel dizzy and disoriented.
On the roundabout of life, I feel tormented.
At heart, I am an eccedentesiast,
hiding pain behind a smile,
I pretend nothing is wrong,
but I obsess over where I belong.
I feel like I am sliding further down.
Regrets fill my head and the decisions of my life
swing in front of me, their weight like lead.
I immerse myself fearlessly in flashbacks but,
I'm about to crack.
As always, I turn up the sound
because my sanity is bound to my girls
with white silk ribbons.

Inner Child

My inner child is happiest
when she hears the first bars of Arrival.
Flares and sequins are the dress code of people
all around.
The theatre lights go down.
My crowned girls are zipping their boots,
ribbons tied.
Inside I have butterflies, the sensation of elation.
I inhale the scent of anticipation
I wait to be 8 years old again.
The healing of my wounds is imminent.
My soul, waiting for 'My My'.

Valentine's Day

(a backwards forwards poem)

On our night of romance
I will pierce your heart with Cupid's arrow.
I'm certain, I taste forever on your lips
when I dream about you.
I've missed you more than I ever thought
imaginable.
My whole body aches for you.
Just one more kiss,
my one wish, for Valentine's Day.

My one wish for Valentine's Day?
Just one more kiss.
My whole body aches for you.
I've missed you more than I ever thought
imaginable.
When I dream about you,
I am certain I taste forever on your lips.
I will pierce your heart with Cupid's arrow,
on our night of romance.

Bubble

I long for our bubble.
An impenetrable iridescent barrier
between our endless love and the outside world.
Our hurdles hidden by haze
in the emerald hues of our bubble space.
As sunlight reflects from your amber eyes,
I feel my love defy gravity because with you,
my reality is a fairytale.
Here we'll stay, until your scent has become
etched into my soul.
Here we'll stay, until I have kissed the whole of
you, over and over again.
Then, we will just be.
Legs entwined and our bubble will shine.
I know that you should not be defined by love,
you should hold your own heart,
but from the start, I wanted our hearts to beat as
one.
So please in this world full of darkness, choose
to be my sun.

Songbird

My Songbird.
The wordsmith I aspired to be
with 'You are everything to me'.
Equally the poet in my heart
and the queen of rock and roll.
You articulated true love from your soul,
like noone else could.
I felt like you understood.

'You Make Loving Fun' always makes me
reminisce
about my first kiss.
In Wickhambreaux we visited your local, had a
few wines
and well, the rest of that evening was nothing
short of divine.
And you wrote the memory for me..
'the feel of your lips on mine'.

Thank you for everything you've left behind.
My current tipple of choice is Friend.
It sums up your journey's end
"When the sun goes down, and you're not
around".
You're my Northern Star in the night,

Christine Perfect, sleep tight.

Christine McVie RIP 1943-2022 Love you.

Take Me Back In Time

I wish for one more Christmas, as an innocent
child.
When Christmas was magical, beyond our
wildest dreams.
Screams of delight filled the house when we saw
the presents under the tree.
You see, you don't realise that the magic fades
over the decades.
One more time with my brother putting out the
mince pie.
One more time laughing until we cried tears of
joy at Nan's ridiculous tales.
One more time of hearing her list all of the
males on her fancy list
and finishing it with "I am not dead yet you
know".
Now that isn't true. Mrs Pearce, you're forever in
my heart.
Oh and you know the soup you wanted to start,
Christmas day 2008?
I have a confession...
It was just a cup a soup with some croutons for
artistic impression.
And Mum, I love you, but your trifle is grim.

Trifle fingers and tinned strawberries belong in
the bin,
but it never mattered because we were full to the
brim.
(of Quality Street from the tin).
Pulling crackers, telling jokes,
when my tipple was nothing more than a can of
coke.
One more time of all of my loved ones around,
before we had to visit Nan in the ground.
I wish for one more time being in that house that
I called home,
at a time when I was loved and didn't feel alone.

You Own My Heart

Last night I had a dream.
I was holding you close, your skin on mine,
our legs entwined.
You whispered 'I love you'.
In these blissful moments
we were reunited and my love was not
unrequited.
This connection I have with you,
it makes me feel like you're an extension of my
own soul.
The distance between us feels like an illusion.
I've seen our lives develop with mirrored
synchronicity
and I wonder whether you too feel the way I do.
Do you dream of our halcyon days?
I am determined to make you mine,
whatever it takes, however long,
because I believe we belong together.
There is an ache in my soul for you
and I am starting to think I will sacrifice
everything for you.
My soul mate.
You own my heart.

The Glass Slipper

Under darkening dusky skies,
I breathe in the sighs of celestial smoke,
to evoke iridescent images, magical memories.
Even allowing for the rosy haze of time,
and the certainty that love can be blind
the words "I love you, be with me?"
are never far from my mind.
When I am found by sleep,
I have dreams of consummating my deepest,
darkest desires.
I wish my life was a book.
then I'd turn to the epilogue,
desperate to take a look to see if
the protagonist has her fairytale ending.
Is the right foot wearing the glass slipper?
Or am I still living through platforms and glitter.
Am I still wearing the mask of a marionette?
Do I have a life full of regret?

Your Embrace

The feeling of defeat spreads.
My legs are heavy, like lead.
I have no motivation.
A sense of stagnation.
I am trapped.
There are arms wrapped around me so tightly, I
am unable to speak.
It is then I know, I will spend a lifetime wishing
for what my inner child seeks.
Loneliness isn't an absence of being surrounded
by people, it's absence of connection.
No doubt also an absence of life direction.
I am futile in my search for both.
I loathe this continual notion of searching for
where I belong,
for somewhere I don't feel wrong.
I search for a place that I feel safe.
Why does this always lead me back to your
embrace?

So Close To The End

The twinkle gone from your eye,
the spark smothered in your heart,
society teems with technology,
yet we feel so far apart.

You searched for ways to numb the pain,
increasingly desperate to find yourself again.
The alcohol swimming round your head
become the monster in your bed.
You got through the day being narcotized,
a party animal in disguise.

But one day, that snuff, it wasn't enough.

So you stood on the edge, 200 feet high,
empty and exhausted and ready to die.

Now I see you with your stitches and wounds
and,
I thank God, you weren't taken too soon.

London

You are not merely a verse in my poem.
You are the crucial chords underpinning the
melody of my life.
You are an ear worm.
A song that I will never forget.
My insecurities make me question whether I
have plagiarised perceptions of you.
I wonder if my feelings are falsely formed from
nostalgic notions and words of love.
Both, eagerly embellished by articulate art of
imagination.
One thing I don't doubt, my heart will spend
forever trying to beat to the same rhythm as
yours, London.

www.ingramcontent.com/pod-product-compliance
Lightning Source LLC
La Vergne TN
LVHW010859200726
843508LV00012B/2938